Mystery Meals

Sleuthing your way through a meal...

Copyright © 2011 CQ Products
Waverly, IA 50677
All rights reserved.
No part of this book may be reproduced or transmitted in any form or by any means, electronic or mechanical, including photocopying, recording or by any information storage and retrieval system, without permission in writing from the publisher.

Printed in the United States of America
by G&R Publishing Co.

Distributed By:

CQ Products

507 Industrial Street
Waverly, IA 50677

ISBN-13: 978-1-56383-411-0
ISBN-10: 1-56383-411-1
Item #7065

Table of Contents

What is a Mystery Meal?...........................4

Mexican Fiesta..8

Wild West..14

Classic Rock..20

Tropical Luau..24

Mardi Gras..30

Lucky in Love...36

Shipwreck Island....................................40

Haunted Halloween...............................46

Fairy Tales...52

*Corresponding menus found
at the back of the book*

What is a Mystery Meal?

It's a deliciously fun way to feed guests and entertain everyone at the same time! Foods from a themed menu are served in three or four separate courses and guests must look at the menu and select the items they wish to eat for each course.

But there's a trick to it. Guests have no idea what foods are being served at the meal because the items on the menu are listed by fictitious code names. Though the code names may offer hints and cryptic clues to a food's identity, guests really have no idea what they are choosing to eat. It's a challenge to figure out what each item might be and choose foods in a "normal" order. But it remains a **MYSTERY** until the food is actually served.

To make it even more entertaining, eating utensils, napkins and toothpicks are listed by fake names too. That means if guests do not order a fork or other tool for each course of their meal, they'll have to eat some foods with their fingers — or use their ingenuity to create a make-shift utensil from something else, such as celery sticks, chips or a folded paper plate. Since the table is cleared after each course, good manners are not required at mystery meals, and that's part of the fun.

This book provides every detail you need to plan and host nine different mystery meals. Each meal will serve eight guests with enough food left over to feed several helpers. Follow these tips and pointers for a hilarious dining adventure with friends.

The plan

- Make a guest list of 8 people who would enjoy this type of party. (Requirements: must love sleuthing and bring a good sense of humor to the table.)
- Pick the party theme and menu you wish to prepare.
- Choose a date. Send invites with RSVPs.
- Decide how you'll decorate. Find, borrow or purchase themed décor. (Use the suggestions provided with each menu or come up with your own ideas.)
- Enlist one or more helpers in the kitchen to dish up and serve food to guests and clear the table after each course. Trays are helpful, but not necessary.
- If you wish to change the menu, now is the time to do it. Alter guest menus accordingly.

The supplies

- Buy the groceries needed for each item on the chosen menu. Compile your list using the recipes and the "Food Prep" directions. (Each theme has two or more recipes with ingredient lists; the remaining items needed are ready-to-use or quick-to-fix foods.)

- Gather multiple serving dishes for each guest because they'll need at least one new plate for each course. For easy clean-up, purchase disposable plates, bowls, cups, Dixie cups, drinking glasses, utensils and napkins to match the theme.
- Photocopy the matching themed menu page from the back of this book for guests to order their foods. Make two copies for each guest before the party.
- Keep this book in the kitchen for a handy reference or make a master list for yourself.

The set-up

- Place the dining table so guests cannot see into the kitchen or discover the foods being prepared – no peeking allowed! Decorate table as desired, adding salt and pepper shakers. Do not set table with any dishes or utensils*.
- Organize the serving area in your kitchen to make it convenient and easy.
- Set stacks of plates (small and large), bowls, cups, glasses and other required serving dishes in a convenient spot. Servers may be able to put all ordered items on one plate for a guest, or they may need to use several different dishes, depending upon what is ordered. For example, if pieces of dessert are already plated, a server may need to deliver two different plates to the guest for one course.
- Reserve a different spot in the work area for each menu item. Forks, knives and spoons should each get their own small spot. Plan to serve food items closest to the area where they were prepared, such as reserving the stovetop area to serve foods cooked in the oven.
- Make a label for every item on the menu, listing the code name, real name and its serving size. Place each label near its namesake in the serving area.
- Place correct measuring cups, spoons or scoops near each food as needed to measure serving sizes. (This is to make sure you don't run out of food. If one serving of baked beans is ½ cup, servers should use a ½ cup measure when dishing up the beans.)
- Assign tasks to the servers and go over the plan together. It's easiest if each server delivers and clears dishes for the same guests throughout the meal.

  *To be a good host, always consider your guest list. If guests will be uncomfortable eating with their hands, you may provide one utensil at the beginning of the meal and allow them to keep it throughout their dining experience, or let them "barter" with other guests to get items they need.

Meal preparation

- Become familiar with the menu and plan your meal prep schedule, allowing enough time to complete all cooking and food prep before guests arrive.
- Do as much ahead of time as possible.
- Prepare refrigerated or frozen dishes at least one day before the party and store accordingly.
- Dish up any items that are self-contained. For example, scoop individual servings of ice cream into bowls and place in the freezer until mealtime. Cut and plate the dessert or salad, cover and store appropriately until serving. When a guest orders those items, the server can grab them and go.
- Serve hot foods hot and cold foods cold. Use ice-filled coolers to increase refrigerator space, and keep food warm in the oven or slow cooker.
- Place ice water and glasses on the table for guests to drink anytime.

Inviting guests to the table

1. **Seat the guests.** Give each person a pencil and menu. Ask them to write their name on their menu.

2. **Explain these things:**
    a. Guests will be served a wonderful meal and they'll eat it together, one course at a time. Everyone will finish the course before the next one is served.
    b. Everyone will eat the same foods, but they may not get the same food at the same time. They will be ordering the food they want for each course, but may drink water throughout the meal.
    c. They can order food from the menu in whatever order they like, but they will be served only the items they selected for each course. (This includes silverware, napkin and beverages!) Don't give any hints about the foods you are serving. The theme and aromas might tip them off, but keep them guessing.
    d. They must order each item on the menu, but use it only once – no duplicates, no skips. They should write down the name of each item on the blanks in the order they wish to receive them. (They can cross off items as they choose them.) When they've made their selections, give them a second menu to make an exact copy of the first one.

3. **Collect one completed menu** from each guest and tell them to keep the duplicate menu so they can refer to it during the meal. Then let the fun begin!

Serving the food

Using the menus that were turned in and the labels in the kitchen, servers should dish up only the food and other items each guest ordered for the first course and then deliver it to the table. Food from the oven or refrigerator should be dished up just before service to maintain its optimal temperature. While guests enjoy their food (or lack of food), they can look at their duplicate menu to figure out what the code names represent.

As guests eat, servers may start dishing up the second course. But please allow plenty of time for guests to savor each course (and chuckle), and don't clear the table or serve the next course until everyone is finished with the previous one. This just adds to the fun! Servers may eat after the meal.

Alter the menu or serving plan as you wish. For example:

- Use scrapbooking materials to create restaurant-style menus.
- Prepare and serve alternate foods and change guest menus as needed.
- If guests are dressed up nicely, rethink the "no utensils" rule.
- Once it has been ordered, let guests keep a utensil for the remaining courses.
- Let guests "earn" a fork, spoon or knife if they sing, dance or share another theme-related stunt. (Hula, anyone?)
- Allow guests to order their food as a group after discussing and "breaking" the code names. (In this manner, only one menu needs to be completed and turned in, and all guests will be served the same goofed-up courses at the same time.)
- After all courses have been served, set out the "leftovers" so guests can have a second helping.

Increase the fun factor!

Toss proper etiquette out the window and just enjoy the silliness!

Mexican Fiesta!

What's for dinner?   A.K.A.

8 guests

What's for dinner?	A.K.A.
Chips & Salsa	Salty Dance
Chips & Guacamole	Pitted Out
Chicken Enchilada Casserole	Chick Under a Poncho
Lettuce, Tomatoes, Green Onions & Sour Cream	Mexican Flag
Pinto Bean Salad	Dressed Pony
Sopapilla Cheesecake Dessert	Sweet Soap
Margarita	Tipsy Sombrero
Mexican Hot Chocolate	Beans & Bark
Fork	Cactus
Knife	Zorro
Spoon	Shared Siesta
Napkin	Matador's Cape

Make 2 copies of matching menu for each guest *(back of book)*

8

Dónde es la fiesta?

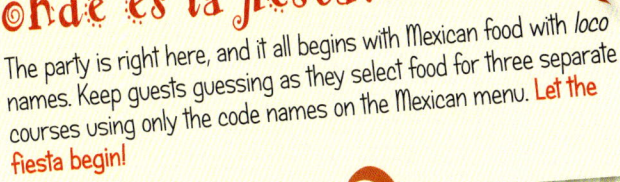

The party is right here, and it all begins with Mexican food with *loco* names. Keep guests guessing as they select food for three separate courses using only the code names on the Mexican menu. **Let the fiesta begin!**

Food Prep **Day Before**

Pinto Bean Salad (Dressed Pony): Make salad, page 10. Cover and chill overnight.

Sopapilla Cheesecake Dessert (Sweet Soap): Prepare dessert, page 13. Cover and chill overnight.

Food Prep **Party Day**

Chicken Enchilada Casserole (Chick Under a Poncho): Assemble and bake casserole, page 11.

Lettuce, Tomatoes, Green Onions & Sour Cream (Mexican Flag): Chop 2 tomatoes and 1 bunch green onions. Toss with 1 bag shredded lettuce; cover and chill. You'll also need 8 oz. sour cream for serving.

Chips & Guacamole (Pitted Out): Using 2 avocados and a 1-oz. envelope guacamole seasoning, make guacamole by following directions on envelope; cover and chill. You'll also need a 13-oz. bag tortilla chips.

Chips & Salsa (Salty Dance): Divide 16 oz. chunky salsa among 8 small serving cups; chill. You'll also need a 13-oz. bag tortilla chips.

Mexican Hot Chocolate (Beans & Bark): Prepare hot chocolate, page 12; keep warm in a slow cooker.

Margarita (Tipsy Sombrero): Just before serving time, blend margaritas, page 12, omitting or adding tequila as appropriate.

Don't Forget

✓ Photocopy menu *(2 per guest)*
✓ Decorate table
✓ Make a label for each menu item *(real name plus code name)*
✓ Organize food service area

9

Dish it Up

Collect one completed Mexican Fiesta menu from each guest. Dish up only one course at a time using this guide to determine serving sizes:

Chips & Salsa: about 5 tortilla chips, 1 small serving cup salsa

Chips & Guacamole: about 5 tortilla chips, 2-3 tablespoons guacamole

Chicken Enchilada Casserole: 1 piece

Lettuce, Tomato, Green Onion mixture: generous ⅓ cup topped with 1-2 tablespoons sour cream

Pinto Bean Salad: ½ cup

Cheesecake Dessert: 1 piece

Margarita: 6-8 ounces

Hot Chocolate: 6-8 ounces

Recipes

Serves 10

Pinto Bean Salad (Dressed Pony)

- 1 tsp. minced garlic
- 3 T. lime juice
- 2 tsp. salt
- ¼ tsp. chili powder
- ¼ C. olive oil
- 1 (16 oz.) can reduced sodium pinto beans, drained, rinsed
- 1⅓ C. corn kernels
- 1 orange or yellow bell pepper, seeded, diced
- ¼ C. chopped red onion
- 1 C. cherry tomatoes, quartered
- ¼ C. chopped fresh cilantro
- ½ C. diced cucumber
- Salt and pepper to taste

In a small bowl, mix garlic, lime juice, salt and chili powder. Gradually whisk in oil to make dressing.

In a large bowl, combine beans, corn, bell pepper and onion. Add dressing and toss to coat. Fold in tomatoes, cilantro and cucumber. Season with salt and pepper. Cover and chill until mealtime.

★ **Note:** If desired, add diced avocado to salad just before serving.

Recipes

Serves 12

Chicken Enchilada Casserole
(Chick Under a Poncho)

- 2 T. vegetable oil
- 1 onion, diced
- 1 green bell pepper, seeded, diced
- 1 (10 oz.) can enchilada sauce
- 2 (10.75 oz.) cans cream of chicken soup
- 1 (4 oz.) can chopped green chiles
- 2 lbs. cooked, shredded chicken, divided
- 2 C. shredded Cheddar cheese, divided
- 2 C. shredded Monterey Jack cheese, divided
- Chicken broth
- 12 corn tortillas

Coat a 9 x 13" baking dish with nonstick cooking spray. In a large skillet over medium heat, heat oil. Add onion and bell pepper and sauté until tender. In a large bowl, stir together enchilada sauce, soups, and green chiles. In a saucepan, heat a small amount of chicken broth. Dip tortillas in warm broth, one at a time, to soften. Arrange a layer of 6 tortillas over the bottom of prepared dish. Spread half the chicken over the tortillas. Pour half the sauce mixture over chicken; top with half the Cheddar cheese and half the Monterey Jack cheese. Repeat the layers of tortillas, chicken, sauce and cheeses. Bake about 30 minutes or until bubbly. Cut into pieces to serve. Garnish with lettuce, tomatoes, green onions and sour cream as desired.

⭐ **Do-ahead tip:** After baking, cut in serving pieces and keep warm in oven until serving.

Who needs an excuse for a fiesta?

Recipes

Margarita (Tipsy Sombrero)

Serves 10

1 (1.75 L) bottle margarita mix
Crushed ice
Tequila, optional

Coarse salt
Fresh lime wedges

Using a blender, follow directions on margarita mix bottle to blend crushed ice and margarita mix until smooth and thick. Add tequila, if desired. Serve in salt-rimmed stemmed glasses with lime wedge.

⭐ **Do-ahead tip:** After blending, place pitcher in the freezer to keep cold.

Mexican Hot Chocolate
(Beans & Bark)

Serves 10

6 oz. semi-sweet baking chocolate, chopped
2 T. sugar
1 to 2 tsp. ground cinnamon

8 C. milk
1 tsp. vanilla extract
Dash of almond extract
Whipped cream, optional

In a blender container or food processor, combine chocolate, sugar and cinnamon. Cover and blend until finely ground. In a large saucepan over low heat, combine chocolate mixture and milk. Stir and cook until chocolate melts. Remove from heat; stir in vanilla and almond extract.

Just before serving, beat with a rotary beater until frothy. Pour into small mugs. Top with whipped cream, if desired.

⭐ **Do-ahead tip:** After cooking, transfer hot mixture to a slow cooker to keep warm until serving time.

Recipes

Serves 12

Sopapilla Cheesecake Dessert
(Sweet Soap)

- 3 (8 oz.) pkgs. cream cheese, softened
- 2 C. sugar, divided
- 1½ tsp. vanilla extract
- 2 (8 oz.) cans refrigerated crescent roll dough
- ½ C. butter, melted
- 1 tsp. ground cinnamon
- ¼ C. sliced almonds
- Honey

Preheat oven to 350°. In a medium mixing bowl, combine cream cheese, 1½ cups sugar and vanilla; beat on medium speed until smooth. Unroll one can of dough and place in a 9 x 13″ baking dish. Flatten dough, sealing perforations. Spread cream cheese mixture evenly over crust in dish. Unroll second can of dough and flatten into a 9 x 13″ rectangle, sealing perforations. Place rectangle over filling to cover. Drizzle melted butter over the top. In a small bowl, mix remaining ½ cup sugar with cinnamon. Sprinkle over melted butter. Top with almonds. Bake about 45 minutes or until dough is puffed and golden brown. Drizzle warm dessert with honey. Cool completely before cutting into squares.

⭐ **Do-ahead tip:** Before mealtime, cut and plate each piece for easy serving; may stand at room temperature for about 1 hour.

Embrace the theme

★ Decorate your dining area with the festive red, green and white colors of the Mexican flag. Fill terra cotta pots, straw baskets or brightly colored pottery with real or silk flowers such as red geraniums. Decorate with sombreros, balloons, piñatas and paper Mexican flags. Hang white and green streamers and strings of mini lights.

★ Cover the serving table with red or green tablecloths or Mexican blankets. For musical fun, arrange instruments such as maracas, bongo drums and castanets nearby and play soft mariachi music in the background. Then start the fiesta!

Wild West

What's for dinner?	A.K.A.
Pigs in a Blanket	Squealing Bedrolls
Jalapeño Poppers	Smokin' Guns
Beef Brisket	Rustler's Game
Baked Beans	Rootin' Tootin' Cowboy
Cinnamon Applesauce	Trigger's Old Age Treat
Corn on the Cob	Chew on This
Biscuits with Honey	Saddlesore & Salve
Butter	Panning for Gold
Peach Cobbler	Boot Fruit
Root Beer (and/or Beer)	Underground Tap
Coffee	Cowboy Joe
Fork	Pitch It
Knife	Whittle a Little
Spoon	Big Dipper
Napkin	Slop Stopper

8 guests

Make 2 copies of matching menu for each guest *(back of book)*

Stampede at OK Corral

Round up the cowboys and gals for a rootin' tootin' tasty meal. There's plenty of western-style grub to go around, but guests will be scratchin' their noggins to figure out what the foods are 'cause confounding nicknames won't give 'em away. They'll choose foods for four separate courses. Gear up for a good time, buckaroos!

Food Prep **Day Before**

Jalapeno Poppers (Smokin' Guns): Assemble poppers, page 17, and freeze until party day.

Root Beer (Underground Tap): Chill 2 liters root beer. Pour into glasses to serve.

Butter (Panning for Gold): Cut butter into 8 generous pats; chill.

Cinnamon Applesauce (Trigger's Old Age Treat): Dish up ½ C. servings of purchased cinnamon applesauce in small cups; cover and chill. You'll need 45-50 oz. applesauce.

Food Prep **Party Day**

Beef Brisket (Rustler's Game): Start cooking brisket 6-7 hours before party, page 18. Slice before serving.

Peach Cobbler (Boot Fruit): Bake cobbler, page 19.

Pigs in a Blanket (Squealing Bedrolls): Assemble appetizers, page 16, and chill. Bake just before mealtime.

Biscuits with Honey (Saddlesore & Salve): Bake refrigerated biscuits following package directions (1-2 per guest). Serve warm with honey.

Coffee (Cowboy Joe): Brew 8-10 cups coffee and keep hot.

Baked Beans (Rootin' Tootin' Cowboy): Heat 3 (16 oz.) cans prepared baked beans; keep warm.

Corn on the Cob (Chew on This): Just before mealtime, cook 1 cob of corn for each guest; keep warm.

Jalapeño Poppers (Smokin' Guns): Just before serving, fry or bake frozen jalapeño poppers, page 17.

Don't Forget

- ✓ Photocopy menu *(2 per guest)*
- ✓ Decorate table
- ✓ Make a label for each menu item *(real name plus code name)*
- ✓ Organize food service area

Dish it Up

Collect one completed Wild West menu from each guest. Dish up only one course at a time using this guide to determine serving sizes:

Pigs in a Blanket: 2-3 appetizers with spoonful of sauce

Jalapeño Poppers: 2-3 poppers

Beef Brisket: several slices

Baked Beans: ½ cup

Cinnamon Applesauce: ½ cup

Corn on the Cob: 1 cob

Biscuits with Honey: 1 or 2 biscuits, about 1 tablespoon honey

Butter: 1 pat

Peach Cobbler: about ½ cup

Root Beer (and/or Beer): 8-12 ounces

Coffee: 6-8 ounces

Recipes

Serves 10

Pigs in a Blanket (Squealing Bedrolls)

⅔ C. Dijon mustard
⅓ C. honey
7 (6″) flour tortillas

1 (14 oz.) pkg. cocktail links ("little smokies")

Line a baking sheet with aluminum foil; spray with cooking spray. Preheat oven to 350°. In a small bowl, mix mustard and honey. Lightly spread mustard mixture over each tortilla; reserve remaining mixture for dipping. Slice each tortilla into six strips. Roll one strip around each link and secure with toothpick. Place on prepared baking sheet and bake for 5 to 8 minutes or until hot. Serve with reserved sauce.

Do-ahead tip: Assemble rolls, cover and refrigerate until baking.

Recipes

Jalapeño Poppers (Smokin' Guns)

Serves 10

- 12 oz. fresh jalapeño peppers
- 12 oz. cream cheese, softened
- 1 (8 oz.) pkg. shredded Cheddar or Monterey Jack cheese
- 1 T. bacon bits
- 1 C. flour
- ½ tsp. garlic powder, or to taste
- Salt and pepper to taste
- 1 C. milk
- 1 C. dry bread crumbs

Protect hands with kitchen gloves. Cut peppers in half lengthwise and remove all or most seeds, depending on heat desired. In a medium bowl, mix cream cheese, Cheddar cheese and bacon bits. Spoon mixture into pepper halves.

In a small bowl, mix flour, garlic powder, salt and pepper. Place milk in another bowl. Dip filled peppers into milk and then into flour mixture, coating well. Allow coated peppers to dry for 10 minutes. Dip peppers in milk again and roll them through bread crumbs; let dry. Dip again in milk and bread crumbs; let dry.

To bake, preheat oven to 350°. Arrange coated peppers in a single layer on a baking sheet and bake for 30 to 40 minutes or until golden brown. Sprinkle warm poppers with salt.

To fry, fill a medium skillet with enough vegetable oil to cover peppers. Heat oil to 365° and deep-fry coated peppers for 2 to 3 minutes, until golden brown. Drain poppers on paper towels; sprinkle with salt.

Do-ahead tip: Make and freeze poppers ahead of time. If frozen before frying, remove from freezer and deep-fry until golden (no thawing required). If frozen after frying, reheat in a 425° oven for 15 minutes.

Always drink upstream from the herd.

Cuz that thar's jus good common sense!

Recipes

Grilled Beef Brisket
(Rustler's Game)

Serves 10

1¼ C. finely chopped onion, divided
2 tsp. paprika
½ tsp. pepper
6 to 8 lbs. boneless beef brisket
2 C. steak sauce, divided

2 T. butter
1 C. ketchup
1 T. brown sugar
¼ tsp. red pepper flakes

Using an outdoor grill, build a low-heat fire with charcoal briquettes or preheat gas grill to low heat. In a small bowl, mix ¾ cup onion, paprika and pepper. Rub mixture evenly over brisket. Place brisket fat side up in large disposable pan. Add ½ cup water and cover tightly with aluminum foil. Set pan on grate over coals, close lid and cook for 5 hours, turning brisket over every 1½ hours. Use a baster to remove accumulating fat in pan; add ½ cup water to pan. Add charcoal briquettes as needed to maintain even temperature.

Remove brisket from pan and set beef directly on grill. Remove and reserve 1 cup of pan drippings. To remaining drippings in pan, stir in 1 cup steak sauce; brush mixture over brisket. Close grill lid and cook for 1 hour, brushing occasionally with sauce and turning once.

Meanwhile, in a medium saucepan over medium-low heat, melt butter. Add remaining ½ cup onion and sauté until tender. Stir in remaining 1 cup steak sauce, reserved pan drippings, ketchup, brown sugar and red pepper. Simmer for at least 10 minutes. Serve with sliced brisket.

Note: Brisket may be cooked in a 275° oven for 5 hours and finished on the grill. Hold in warm oven until serving.

Do-ahead tip: Slice cooked brisket ahead of time and keep warm in sauce until serving.

Recipes

Serves 10

Peach Cobbler (Boot Fruit)

½ C. butter
1 C. flour
1½ C. sugar, divided
1 T. baking powder
Pinch of salt

1 C. milk
1 tsp. vanilla or almond extract
4 C. fresh peach slices
1 T. lemon juice
Ground cinnamon or nutmeg

Preheat oven to 375°. In a 9 x 13" baking dish, melt butter. In a medium bowl, combine flour, 1 cup sugar, baking powder and salt. Add milk and vanilla; stir until just blended. Pour batter over butter without stirring.

In a medium saucepan over high heat, combine remaining ½ cup sugar, peaches and lemon juice. Bring to a boil, stirring constantly. Pour mixture over batter without stirring. Sprinkle with cinnamon. Bake for 40 to 45 minutes or until golden brown. Serve warm or cool.

Embrace the theme

Invite guests to dress up as ranch hands, miners or outlaws. Serve food on metal or disposable foil pie pans or silver paper plates. Let guests guzzle cold beverages from mason jars or clean tin cans, and use tin cups, mugs or silver paper cups to serve hot coffee.

Set the table with a red and white checkered tablecloth or old wool blanket. Purchase inexpensive red bandanas for napkins. Set out other western décor such as cowboy hats and boots, small hay bales, old blankets, saddles, horseshoes, gun belts and toy pistols or saloon gear.

Classic Rock

8 guests

What's for dinner?	A.K.A.
Bacon Rolls	It's Only Rock and Roll
Toothpicks	Light My Fire
Lettuce/Dressing	Come Together
Pizza Slice #1	Pick up the Pieces
Pizza Slice #2	American Pie
Parmesan Cheese	Whole Lotta Shakin' Goin' On
Red Pepper Flakes	Hot Fun in the Summertime
Fruit Salad	Tutti Frutti
Ice Cream Sundae	Groovin' on a Sunday Afternoon
Chocolate Chip Cookies	Will It Go Round in Circles
Cola	Black Water
Ice Cubes	Cold as Ice
Knife & Fork	Happy Together
Spoon	Love Bites
Napkin	Wipeout

Make 2 copies of matching menu for each guest (back of book)

20

Rock Out!

Take it Easy and have a rockin' good time with these simple-to-prepare foods. Guests will choose menu items in three courses, using only classic rock and roll song titles as their clues. **Everyone will soon be Feelin' Groovy!**

Food Prep **Day Before**

Ice Cream Sundae (Groovin' on a Sunday Afternoon): Prepare Fudge Sauce, page 23. Buy 1 gal. vanilla ice cream. Put 1-2 scoops in each sundae dish or bowl; cover and freeze overnight.

Ice Cubes (Cold as Ice): 3 per guest.

Chocolate Chip Cookies (Will It Go Round in Circles): Purchase or bake your favorite cookies (1-2 cookies per guest). Store in an airtight container.

Cola (Black Water): Chill 2 L cola.

Food Prep **Party Day**

Fruit Salad (Tutti Frutti): In a large bowl, combine 8 C. fresh fruit (strawberries, blueberries, grapes, pineapple and melon chunks); cover and chill. Before serving, add 2 sliced bananas and toss fruit with 1/3 C. orange juice.

Bacon Rolls (It's Only Rock and Roll): Prepare rolls, page 22. Keep warm until serving.

Pizza (Pick up the Pieces, American Pie): Order carry-out pizza or bake your own (2 slices per guest plus extra for servers). Keep warm until serving.

Lettuce/Dressing (Come Together): Rinse iceberg lettuce; cut 8-10 wedges. Chill on serving plates. To serve, drizzle with any salad dressing.

Cola (Black Water): Serve in glasses (2 L needed).

Ice (Cold as Ice): Pour cola over ice (if ordered together) or serve in a small cup if ordered alone.

Ice Cream Sundae (Groovin' on a Sunday Afternoon): To serve, remove dishes from freezer and top with warm fudge sauce, whipped cream and a cherry.

Don't Forget

✓ Photocopy menu *(2 per guest)*
✓ Decorate table
✓ Make a label for each menu item *(real name plus code name)*
✓ Organize food service area

Dish it Up

Collect one completed Classic Rock menu from each guest. Dish up only one course at a time using this guide to determine serving sizes:

Bacon Rolls: 3-5 rolls

Lettuce/Dressing: 1 wedge, 1-2 tablespoons dressing

Pizza: 1 slice each time it's ordered

Parmesan Cheese: about 1 tablespoon

Red Pepper Flakes: ½-1 teaspoon

Fruit Salad: ¾ cup

Ice Cream Sundae: 1-2 scoops, 2-3 tablespoons fudge sauce

Cookies: 1-2

Cola: 8 ounces

Recipes

Bacon Rolls (It's Only Rock and Roll)

Serves 12

- 1 (12-16 oz.) pkg. thinly sliced bacon
- 2 (8 oz.) cans whole water chestnuts, drained
- ⅓ C. brown sugar
- ⅓ C. mayonnaise
- ⅓ C. chili sauce
- Dash of red pepper sauce, optional

Preheat oven to 350°. Soak wooden toothpicks in water for 20 minutes. Cut each bacon strip in half or thirds. Wrap one bacon piece around each water chestnut; secure with toothpick. Place in shallow baking dish or broiler pan. Bake for 20 to 25 minutes.

Meanwhile, in a small bowl, mix brown sugar, mayonnaise, chili sauce and red pepper sauce, if desired. When rolls are done baking, remove from grease and transfer to a clean shallow baking dish. Pour chili sauce mixture over rolls. Bake for 10 to 20 minutes more or until bacon is crispy. Keep warm until serving.

Do-ahead tip: Wrap water chestnuts in bacon; cover and refrigerate. Prepare sauce and refrigerate. Before serving, bake as directed.

Recipes

Serves 20

Fudge Sauce (Groovin')

1 (12 oz.) can evaporated milk
1 (12 oz.) pkg. semi-sweet chocolate chips (2 C.)
½ C. sugar
1 T. butter
1 tsp. vanilla extract (or mint, raspberry or orange flavoring)

In a large saucepan over medium heat, combine evaporated milk, chocolate chips and sugar; bring to a boil, stirring constantly. Remove from heat. Stir in butter until smooth and creamy. Stir in vanilla. Cool about 30 minutes or until sauce begins to thicken. Serve warm over ice cream. May be covered and refrigerated for up to 1 month.

Do-ahead tip: Make sauce ahead of time and reheat quantity needed in the microwave just before serving.

Embrace The Theme

Roll out trendy 60s, 70s and/or 80s decorations for your party! Use tie-dyed fabric or fabric with a peace sign motif for tablecloths and napkins. Make and display large tissue paper flowers. Print and hang posters of famous rock and roll groups or solo musicians. Display old vinyl albums and 45s with or without their covers. Hang crepe paper streamers in neon colors. Scatter large plump pillows around on the floor. For added ambiance, turn on a strobe or black light.

Invite guests to wear tie-dyed t-shirts, old blue jeans or bell-bottoms, flip flops, leather headbands, floppy hats, newsboy hats, wire-rimmed colored sunglasses, mood rings and peace sign jewelry. Of course, they should fix their hair or wear wigs appropriate to the era.

TROPICAL LUAU

What's for dinner?   A.K.A.

What's for dinner?	A.K.A.
Maui Onion Dip/Chips	Dip in the Rip
Macadamia Nuts	Imitation Pearls
Piña Colada	Do the Rumba
Sweet & Sour Chicken	Opposites Attract
Brown Rice	Grains of Sand
Fresh Fruit Skewers	Sweet Spit
Banana Bread	Monkey Money
Hawaiian Punch	Island Fight
Coconut-Caramel Dessert	Chillin' on the Beach
Fork & Spoon	Two Tickets to Paradise
Napkin	Lei in Lap
Toothpick	Tiki Time

8 guests

Make 2 copies of matching menu for each guest *(back of book)*

24

ALOHA!

Step into a tropical paradise and serve three courses of a delectable Hawaiian-themed meal. Code names challenge guests with island beach clues. Just relax and enjoy the warmth of good friends and great food.

TROPICAL LUAU

Food Prep **Day Before**

Maui Onion Dip/Chips (Dip in the Rip): Mix onion dip, page 26; cover and chill. Serve with rippled potato chips.

Banana Bread (Monkey Money): Bake and cool banana bread, page 28. Before serving, slice and butter as desired.

Hawaiian Punch (Island Fight): Chill ½ gal. Hawaiian Punch. Serve over ice, or if preferred, whisk in 4 C. pineapple sherbet and 1 qt. ginger ale before serving.

Coconut-Caramel Dessert (Chillin' on the Beach): Prepare dessert, page 29; freeze overnight.

Food Prep **Party Day**

Macadamia Nuts (Imitation Pearls): Place 1 oz. nuts in each nut cup.

Sweet & Sour Chicken (Opposites Attract): Start preparing chicken 1½-2 hours before mealtime, page 27. Keep warm to serve.

Brown Rice (Grains of Sand): Follow package directions to prepare at least ½ C. cooked rice per guest. Keep warm.

Fresh Fruit Skewers (Sweet Spit): Slide bite-size fresh fruit chunks (pineapple, melon, strawberries, grapes) onto 10" bamboo skewers (1 per guest). Chill until serving.

Coconut-Caramel Dessert (Chillin' on the Beach): Before mealtime, cut dessert and plate each piece; return to freezer until serving.

Piña Colada (Do the Rumba): Blend coladas, page 27, omitting or adding rum as appropriate.

Don't Forget

✓ Photocopy menu *(2 per guest)*
✓ Decorate table
✓ Make a label for each menu item *(real name plus code name)*
✓ Organize food service area

Dish it Up

Collect one completed Tropical Luau menu from each guest. Dish up only one course at a time using this guide to determine serving sizes:

Onion Dip/Chips: 2-3 tablespoons dip, about 10 potato chips

Macadamia Nuts: 1 ounce

Piña Colada: 6-8 ounces

Sweet & Sour Chicken: 1 piece

Brown Rice: ½ cup

Fruit Skewers: 1 skewer

Banana Bread: 1 buttered slice

Punch: 8 ounces

Coconut-Caramel Dessert: 1 piece

Recipes

Maui Onion Dip (Dip in the Rip)

Serves 12

- 2 T. olive oil
- 2 Vidalia or Maui onions, halved and thinly sliced
- 1 C. sour cream
- ½ C. buttermilk
- 1 tsp. salt
- Rippled potato chips

In a large nonstick skillet over medium heat, heat oil. Add onions and cook about 20 minutes, stirring occasionally, until browned and tender. If necessary, reduce heat and add 1 tablespoon water. Transfer onions to a small bowl and chill about 1 hour.

Using a food processor or blender, pulse onions, sour cream, buttermilk and salt until just combined. Transfer to a bowl, cover and chill at least 1 hour. Serve with potato chips.

Do-ahead tip: Dip can be made and chilled up to 2 days ahead of time.

Recipes

Serves 10

PIÑA COLADA (Do the Rumba)

1½ C. cream of coconut, divided
1 C. crushed pineapple, divided
3 C. pineapple juice, divided
4 to 6 C. crushed ice, divided
Rum, optional
Maraschino cherries, pineapple wedges

In a blender container, combine ¾ cup cream of coconut, ½ cup crushed pineapple, 1½ cups juice and 2-3 cups ice; blend until smooth. Add rum, if desired. Divide among 4-5 glasses. Garnish with a maraschino cherry and pineapple wedge. Repeat to make a second batch.

Do-ahead tip: After blending, place pitcher in the freezer to keep cold.

Serves 10

SWEET & SOUR CHICKEN
(Opposites Attract)

10 boneless, skinless
   chicken breast halves
2 eggs, beaten
Cornstarch
Vegetable oil
1½ C. sugar
½ C. ketchup
2 T. soy sauce
1 tsp. garlic powder

Preheat oven to 325°. Dip chicken pieces in egg; roll in cornstarch. In a large skillet over medium heat, heat approximately ½" oil. Fry chicken until lightly browned on both sides. Place chicken in a shallow baking dish. In a small bowl, mix sugar, ketchup, soy sauce and garlic powder. Pour sauce over chicken.

Bake uncovered for 1 hour, basting pieces with sauce several times during cooking. Keep warm to serve.

Recipes

Serves 10

BANANA BREAD (Monkey Money)

1 C. sugar
½ C. butter, softened
2 eggs
3 medium overripe bananas, mashed
2 C. flour
Pinch of salt
1 tsp. baking soda
1 T. milk mixed with ¼ tsp. lemon juice
1 C. chopped pecans or walnuts, optional

Preheat oven to 350°. Grease and flour a standard loaf pan (or 2 smaller ones). In a large mixing bowl, cream sugar and butter on medium speed until smooth. Beat in eggs. Stir in bananas until blended.

In a separate bowl, stir together flour, salt and baking soda; add to banana mixture and beat until blended. Stir in milk mixture. Blend in pecans, if desired. Spread batter in prepared pan and bake standard loaf for 55 to 60 minutes or until bread tests done with a toothpick. (Shorten baking time for smaller loaves.) Cool 10 minutes before removing from pan to cool completely. Slice before serving.

Lei (lā): a garland of flowers worn around the neck or head

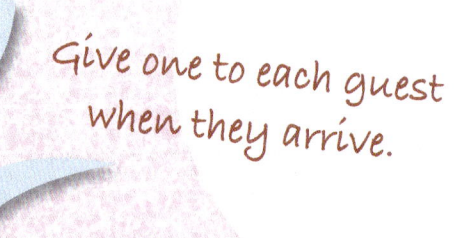

Give one to each guest when they arrive.

Recipes

COCONUT-CARAMEL DESSERT
(Chillin' on the Beach)

Serves 15

- 1½ C. flour
- 2 tsp. baking powder
- ¼ tsp. salt
- 1 C. butter, softened, divided
- 1¼ C. chopped pecans, divided
- 1½ C. sweetened flaked coconut
- 1 (8 oz.) pkg. cream cheese, softened
- 1 (14 oz.) can sweetened condensed milk
- 1 (12 oz.) tub frozen whipped topping, thawed
- 1 (12.25 oz.) jar caramel sauce

Preheat oven to 350°. Lightly coat a 9 x 13" baking pan with cooking spray. In a medium bowl, combine flour, baking powder, salt, ¾ cup butter and ¾ cup pecans until crumbly. Press mixture in prepared pan. Bake for 18 to 20 minutes or until lightly browned; cool.

In a medium saucepan over low heat, melt remaining ¼ cup butter. Add coconut and remaining ½ cup pecans. Cook, stirring often, until coconut is golden; cool.

In a medium mixing bowl, beat cream cheese and sweetened condensed milk on medium speed until smooth. Fold in whipped topping.

Using ⅓ of each mixture, spread layers of cream cheese mixture, caramel sauce and coconut mixture over crust. Repeat layers two more times. Cover pan and freeze overnight. Cut into pieces to serve.

EMBRACE THE THEME

Cover the table with a bright floral or striped tablecloth. Fill vases with fresh or silk flowers, or make tissue paper flowers in bright colors. Hang green streamers around dining area. Decorate with whole coconuts or pineapples and straw baskets filled with sand and sea shells.

Encourage guests to wear tropical-themed clothes and flip-flops. Serve drinks in imitation coconut shells or colored plastic glasses with paper umbrellas. Play Hawaiian music softly in the background.

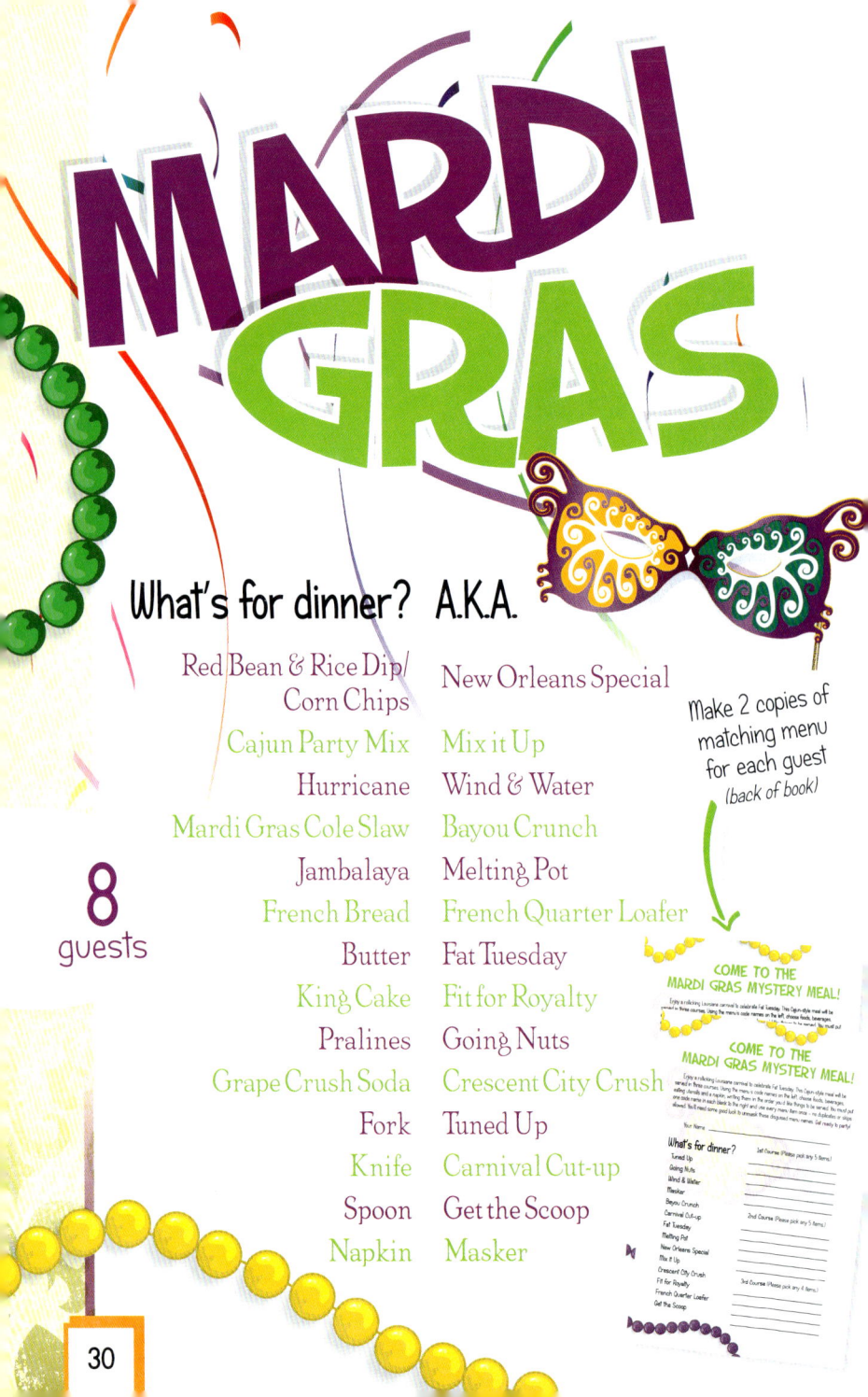

MARDI GRAS

What's for dinner? A.K.A.

8 guests

What's for dinner?	A.K.A.
Red Bean & Rice Dip/Corn Chips	New Orleans Special
Cajun Party Mix	Mix it Up
Hurricane	Wind & Water
Mardi Gras Cole Slaw	Bayou Crunch
Jambalaya	Melting Pot
French Bread	French Quarter Loafer
Butter	Fat Tuesday
King Cake	Fit for Royalty
Pralines	Going Nuts
Grape Crush Soda	Crescent City Crush
Fork	Tuned Up
Knife	Carnival Cut-up
Spoon	Get the Scoop
Napkin	Masker

Make 2 copies of matching menu for each guest (back of book)

COME TO THE MARDI GRAS MYSTERY MEAL!

LET THE GOOD TIMES ROLL!

Fat Tuesday comes once a year, but you can party like it's Mardi Gras anytime with this menu. Serve traditional New Orleans fare in three courses. Code names disguise the food and utensils so it won't be a Big Easy, but with luck, guests will get what they need. **Start the party!**

Food Prep **Day Before**

Red Bean & Rice Dip (New Orleans Special): Mix dip, page 32, but do not bake; cover and chill until party day.

Cajun Party Mix (Mix it Up): Prepare party mix, page 33. Store in an airtight container. Serve in small paper cups.

Mardi Gras Cole Slaw (Bayou Crunch): Prepare dressing mixture, page 33; cover and chill overnight.

Pralines (Going Nuts): Purchase 1 praline for each guest (or make your favorite recipe).

Food Prep **Party Day**

Jambalaya (Melting Pot): Start jambalaya 2-3 hours before guests arrive, page 34. Keep warm.

King Cake (Fit for Royalty): Bake and frost cake, page 35.

Red Bean & Rice Dip/Corn Chips (New Orleans Special): Bake dip, page 32. Serve warm with corn chips.

Mardi Gras Cole Slaw (Bayou Crunch): Cut vegetables; toss with dressing before serving, page 33.

Hurricane (Wind & Water): Mix 4 C. orange juice, 4 C. sour mix, 1 C. passion fruit syrup and 2 T. grenadine. Serve over ice in hurricane glasses; garnish with lime slice. Add rum, if desired.

French Bread (French Quarter Loafer): Heat 1 loaf French bread according to package directions; slice and serve warm.

Butter (Fat Tuesday): Cut butter into 8 generous pats.

Grape Soda (Crescent City Crush): Pour over ice in glasses (2 L needed).

Don't Forget

- ✓ Photocopy menu *(2 per guest)*
- ✓ Decorate table
- ✓ Make a label for each menu item *(real name plus code name)*
- ✓ Organize food service area

Dish it Up

Collect one completed Mardi Gras menu from each guest. Dish up only one course at a time using this guide to determine serving sizes:

Bean & Rice Dip/Chips
3 tablespoons dip,
10 corn chips

Cajun Party Mix: ½ cup

Hurricane: 6-8 ounces
Cole Slaw: about ½ cup
Jambalaya: 1-1½ cups
French Bread: 1 slice

Butter: 1 pat
King Cake: 1 piece
Pralines: 1 piece
Grape Soda: 8 ounces

Recipes

RED BEAN & RICE DIP
(New Orleans Special)

Serves 15

- 1 (8 oz.) pkg. New Orleans style red beans and rice mix
- ½ C. salsa
- 2 T. chopped green onion
- 1 (8 oz.) pkg. cream cheese, softened
- 1½ C. shredded Cheddar cheese, divided
- 1 (14 oz.) pkg. corn chip scoops

Prepare red beans and rice mix as directed on package, but use just 3 cups water. Reserve half of prepared rice mixture for another use.

Preheat oven to 350°. To remaining rice mixture, add salsa, green onion, cream cheese and 1 cup Cheddar cheese; stir until well blended. Pour into a baking dish and sprinkle with remaining ½ cup Cheddar cheese. Bake for 15 to 20 minutes or until hot and bubbly. Keep warm until serving. Serve with corn chips.

Recipes

CAJUN PARTY MIX (Mix it Up)

Serves 12

2 C. each: Cheez-it crackers, pretzels, Crispix cereal
1 C. mixed nuts
6 T. butter, melted
½ tsp. garlic powder
¼ tsp. celery salt
¼ tsp. cayenne pepper
2-3 drops hot pepper sauce

Preheat oven to 250°. In a large roasting pan, combine crackers, pretzels, cereal and nuts. Stir together butter, garlic powder, celery salt, cayenne pepper and pepper sauce; pour over cracker mixture and stir to coat. Bake uncovered for 35 to 40 minutes, stirring every 15 minutes. Cool completely. Store in an airtight container.

MARDI GRAS COLE SLAW (Bayou Crunch)

Serves 12

½ C. apple cider vinegar
⅓ C. brown sugar
1 tsp. dry mustard
2 tsp. celery seed
½ tsp. cayenne pepper
½ tsp. dry dill weed
1 C. sour cream
½ C. mayonnaise
1 tsp. prepared horseradish
Salt to taste
1 head red cabbage, shredded
2 yellow bell peppers, diced
2 zucchini, cut into ¼" strips

In a small bowl, whisk together vinegar, brown sugar, dry mustard, celery seed, cayenne pepper, dill weed, sour cream, mayonnaise, horseradish and salt. Cover and chill overnight.

When ready to serve, combine cabbage, bell peppers and zucchini in a large bowl. Add desired amount of dressing mixture and toss to coat.

Do-ahead tip: Cut up vegetables, cover and refrigerate until mixing.

Recipes

Serves 12

JAMBALAYA (Melting Pot)

- ¼ C. vegetable oil
- 1 (3 lb.) chicken, cut up
- 1 (12 oz.) pkg. andouille sausage, thinly sliced
- 1 tsp. Creole seasoning
- 2 tsp. salt, divided
- 2 onions, chopped
- 2 stalks celery, chopped
- ½ C. chopped green bell pepper
- 3 cloves garlic, minced
- 1 (8 oz.) can tomato sauce
- 1 lb. shrimp, peeled, deveined
- 2 T. chopped fresh parsley
- 2 T. chopped green onion
- 4 C. cooked rice

Place oil in a large heavy pot over medium-high heat. Add chicken pieces and brown on all sides; cook until tender, 20 to 25 minutes. Add sausage, seasoning and 1 teaspoon salt. Cover, reduce heat and cook about 30 minutes or until chicken is well done. Remove chicken and sausage and debone chicken; set both meats aside.

Drain off ⅔ of drippings. To remaining drippings in pot, add onions, celery, bell pepper and garlic; sauté until tender. Stir in tomato sauce, remaining 1 teaspoon salt, chicken, sausage and shrimp. Cover and simmer about 10 minutes, stirring occasionally. Add parsley and green onions; cover and cook for 5 minutes. Fold in cooked rice and simmer until heated through. Keep warm until serving.

Do-ahead tip: Cut onions, celery, bell pepper and garlic; refrigerate in a zippered plastic bag until ready to cook.

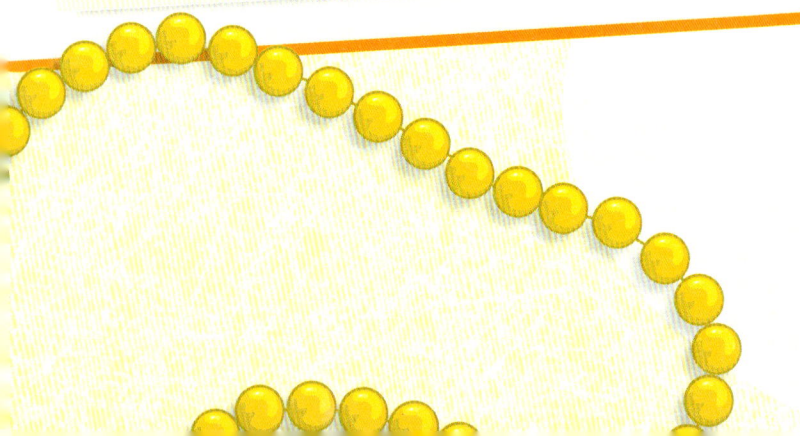

Recipes

KING CAKE (Fit for Royalty)

Serves 12

3 (12-14 oz.) cans refrigerated sweet roll dough (cinnamon or orange) with icing packs
Milk
Green, purple and gold colored sugars
Small plastic baby doll or bean*

Preheat oven to 350°. Lightly grease a baking sheet with cooking spray. Open the cans and separate the sweet rolls; unroll each coil of dough to make 24 strands (about 12" long). Lightly press two strands together, side by side, to make a rope; repeat to make 11 more ropes. Braid three ropes together to make one thick braid; repeat to make three more thick braids. Place the four thick braids on prepared pan, end to end; pinch ends together to make one long, even braid. Shape into an oblong ring, pinching ends together to close ring. Cover loosely with foil and bake until golden brown and firm to the touch, 30 to 40 minutes. Cool on a wire rack.

Cut a slit along the inside of the ring and insert plastic baby doll, pushing it into the cake until hidden. Combine the icing packs and thin with a little milk to reach a drizzling consistency. Drizzle icing over cake. Dust with colored sugars as desired. Cut into pieces to serve.

*The person who finds the doll or bean must provide the next King cake or throw the next party.

EMBRACE THE THEME

Decorate with a purple, gold and green color scheme, using streamers, mini lights, balloons, glow sticks, curly ribbon and tablecloths. Display posters of Mardi Gras festivities and hang up metallic or feather masks.

Serve food using paper plates and cups in metallic gold, purple or green. Scatter foil-covered chocolate coins and confetti on the table along with strands of Mardi Gras beads.

As guests arrive, hand out colored beads, feather masks and/or shiny paper crowns to wear. Play soft jazz music in the background and invite guests to play limbo, charades or other games after the meal.

lucky in love

What's for dinner? A.K.A.

Hot Spinach & Artichoke Dip/Pita Chips	Hot Couple
Sparkling Juice Cocktail*	You Make My Head Spin
Beef Burgundy	Wine & Dine
Noodles	Use It or Lose It
Frozen Fruit Cup	Chilling Out Together
Honey-Glazed Carrots	24 Karat Rings
Knotted Breadsticks	Tie the Knot
Butter	Love Pats
Raspberry-Brownie Dessert	Heart's Desire
Espresso Coffee	Hot & Steamy
Fork	Cupid's Arrow
Knife	Cut to the Chase
Spoon	Cuddling
Napkin	Keep it Clean
Toothpick	"I pick you!"

Or champagne or wine spritzer

Make 2 copies of matching menu for each guest *(back of book)*

8 guests

36

love is in the air

Celebrate love with a romantic meal that's easy to prepare. Guests will choose menu items in three courses, using only lovey-dovey code names for clues. **Turn up the heat with candlelight and romance!**

Food Prep **Day Before**

Raspberry-Brownie Dessert (Heart's Desire): Make dessert, page 39. Cut hearts and plate pieces on party day. Add toppings before serving.

Sparkling Juice Cocktail (You Make My Head Spin): Chill 3 (25 oz.) bottles, any flavor. Serve in stemmed glasses.

Frozen Fruit Cups (Chilling Out Together): Mix 10 oz. thawed sweetened strawberries, 6 oz. thawed pineapple-orange juice concentrate, 20 oz. crushed pineapple, 11 oz. mandarin oranges/juice, 3 diced bananas, 3 T. lemon juice and 8 oz. thawed blueberries. Fill 5-oz. cups and freeze. Thaw slightly before serving.

Food Prep **Party Day**

Beef Burgundy (Wine & Dine): Start beef 8 hours before mealtime, page 38. Keep warm in slow cooker.

Honey-Glazed Carrots (24 Karat Rings): Cook 1 lb. carrot coins until tender. Drain and add 2 T. butter, 2 T. honey and 1 T. lemon juice; cook until glazed, 5 minutes. Serve warm.

Noodles (Use It or Lose It): Cook 2 oz. dry pasta per guest. Toss with olive oil; serve warm.

Knotted Breadsticks (Tie the Knot): Separate refrigerated breadsticks (11 oz. can), cut in half and tie into knots. Bake at 350° for 12-14 minutes or until golden brown; serve warm.

Butter (Love Pats): Cut butter into 8 generous pats.

Hot Spinach-Artichoke Dip (Hot Couple): Mix a 15 oz. jar creamy spinach dip with ½ C. finely chopped artichoke hearts. Heat in the microwave. Serve warm with pita chips (10 oz. needed).

Espresso Coffee (Hot & Steamy): Brew 8-10 cups as desired; keep hot.

Don't Forget

- ✓ Photocopy menu *(2 per guest)*
- ✓ Decorate table
- ✓ Make a label for each menu item *(real name plus code name)*
- ✓ Organize food service area

Dish it Up

Collect one completed Lucky in Love menu from each guest. Dish up only one course at a time using this guide to determine serving sizes:

Spinach & Artichoke Dip/Chips: 2-3 tablespoons dip, 10 pita chips

Juice Cocktail: 8 ounces

Beef Burgundy: about ½ cup

Noodles: 1 cup

Frozen Fruit: 1 small cup

Honey-Glazed Carrots: ½ cup

Knotted Breadsticks: 2-3 knots

Butter: 1 pat

Raspberry-Brownie Dessert: 1 piece

Coffee: 6-8 ounces

Recipes

Serves 10

beef burgundy (Wine & Dine)

- 3 bacon strips, chopped
- 2½ lbs. lean sirloin tip or round steak, cubed
- ⅓ C. flour
- 1 tsp. salt
- 1 tsp. seasoned salt
- ½ tsp. dried marjoram
- ½ tsp. dried thyme
- ¼ tsp. pepper
- 1-2 cloves garlic, minced
- 1 beef bouillon cube, crushed
- 1¼ C. burgundy wine
- ⅓ C. sliced fresh mushrooms
- 2½ T. cornstarch

In a large skillet over medium heat, cook bacon until browned. Remove bacon and reserve drippings. Coat beef with flour and brown on all sides in bacon drippings.

Transfer beef, bacon drippings, cooked bacon, salt, seasoned salt, marjoram, thyme, pepper, garlic, bouillon and wine to a slow cooker. Cover and cook on low for 6 to 8 hours.

Add mushrooms. Dissolve cornstarch in 2½ tablespoons water. Add to slow cooker. Cover and cook on high for 15 minutes. Serve over hot noodles.

Recipes

Serves 12

raspberry-brownie dessert
(Heart's Desire)

1 (19.5 oz.) pkg. milk chocolate brownie mix
½ C. vegetable oil
4 eggs, divided
1 (8 oz.) pkg. cream cheese, softened
½ C. seedless raspberry jam
¼ C. sour cream
1 tsp. vanilla extract
Chocolate or fudge sauce
½ C. fresh raspberries
1 qt. vanilla ice cream

Preheat oven to 350°. Coat a 9 x 13" baking dish with cooking spray. In a large bowl, combine brownie mix, oil, ¼ cup water and 2 eggs; stir until blended. Pour into prepared baking dish.

In a medium mixing bowl, beat cream cheese and jam on medium speed until well mixed. Beat in remaining 2 eggs, sour cream and vanilla to blend. Spread over brownie batter. Bake for 35 to 40 minutes or until edges are golden brown and center is puffed and set when lightly touched. Cool completely.

Using a 2½" to 3" heart-shaped metal cookie cutter, cut at least 8 hearts out of brownies; remove from pan and place on small plates. Before serving, drizzle sauce generously over brownies. Top with raspberries and add a scoop of ice cream on the side.

embrace the theme

Create a romantic ambiance with candlelight, fresh flowers and soft instrumental music playing in the background. Cover the table with a red or pink tablecloth and sprinkle shiny "X", "O" and heart confetti or conversation hearts on top. Hang paper hearts, cupids and old Valentine's Day cards.

For added fun, display black-and-white posters of famous romantic couples from old movies surrounded by red, pink and white balloons. Purchase paper plates, napkins and other décor with a Valentine's Day theme.

Shipwreck Island

What's for dinner? A.K.A.

8 guests

Crab Bites	Grouchy Castaways
Fish Cracker Mix	Fish Bait
Blue Lagoon	Float Your Boat
Stuffed Pasta	Sea Shells
Spinach Salad	Seaweed
Crusty Bread	Sponge
Herbed Dipping Oil	Oil Slick
Pineapple Upside-Down Cake	Sunken Treasure
Ginger Ale	Liquid Gold
Fork	Harpoon
Spoon	Oar
Knife	Swashbuckler
Napkin	Net
Toothpick	Splinter

Make 2 copies of matching menu for each guest *(page 62)*

SOS! Rescued at the Shipwreck Island Mystery Meal!

40

SOS!

A tiny ship has landed on an uncharted desert isle. Come to the rescue and feed the castaways three courses of island-themed food. The code names might make some waves, but guests must use their survival smarts to select the food and utensils they need. **Time to set sail, Matey!**

Food Prep **Day Before**

Crab Bites (Grouchy Castaways): Mix crab filling, page 42; cover and chill. (Finish on party day.)

Fish Cracker Mix (Fish Bait): Combine 11 oz. goldfish crackers, 1 C. peanuts and 1 C. pretzels. Store in an airtight container.

Spinach Salad (Seaweed): Mix salad dressing only, page 44; chill overnight.

Herbed Dipping Oil (Oil Slick): In a shaker jar, mix ¾ C. olive oil, 1½ tsp. Italian herb seasoning, 2 T. Parmesan cheese and pepper to taste. Store at room temperature.

Food Prep **Party Day**

Pineapple Upside-Down Cake (Sunken Treasure): Bake cake, page 45. Reheat as needed to serve.

Stuffed Pasta (Sea Shells): Bake pasta, page 43. Keep warm to serve.

Crusty Bread (Sponge): Bake or reheat 1 loaf crusty bread according to package directions. Slice and serve warm.

Crab Bites (Grouchy Castaways): Fill tart shells and bake, page 42. Serve warm or at room temperature.

Spinach Salad (Seaweed): Assemble salad, page 44; add dressing just before serving.

Blue Lagoon (Float Your Boat): Mix 4 pkgs. blue Kool-aid, 12 oz. frozen lemonade concentrate and 1½ L chilled lemon-lime soda.

Fish Cracker Mix (Fish Bait): Divide among small cups to serve.

Ginger Ale (Liquid Gold): Pour over ice in glasses to serve (2 L needed).

Herbed Dipping Oil (Oil Slick): Pour onto small plates to serve.

Don't Forget

✓ Photocopy menu *(2 per guest)*
✓ Decorate table
✓ Make a label for each menu item *(real name plus code name)*
✓ Organize food service area

Dish it Up

Collect one completed Shipwreck Island menu from each guest. Dish up only one course at a time using this guide to determine serving sizes:

Crab Bites: 2-3 bites

Fish Cracker Mix: about ½ cup

Blue Lagoon: 6 ounces

Stuffed Pasta: 2 stuffed shells

Spinach Salad: about 1 cup

Crusty Bread: 1-2 slices

Herbed Dipping Oil: 1-2 tablespoons

Pineapple Upside-Down Cake: 1 piece

Ginger Ale: 8 ounces

Recipes

Serves 10

Crab Bites (Grouchy Castaways)

- 1 (8 oz.) pkg. cream cheese, softened
- 1 (6 oz.) can crabmeat, drained
- 2 T. mayonnaise
- 2 T. grated Parmesan cheese
- ½ C. shredded Cheddar cheese
- 2 T. thinly sliced green onion
- 1 tsp. Worcestershire sauce
- 30 mini phyllo shells
- Paprika

Preheat oven to 375°. In a large bowl, combine cream cheese, crabmeat, mayonnaise, Parmesan cheese, Cheddar cheese, onion and Worcestershire sauce. Mix well. Spoon about a teaspoonful of mixture into each phyllo shell; sprinkle with paprika. Arrange filled shells on a baking sheet and bake for 15 to 20 minutes or until light brown.

Do-ahead tip: Freeze baked shells and just reheat before serving.

Recipes

Stuffed Pasta (Sea Shells)

Serves 10

- 1½ lbs. large shrimp, peeled, deveined
- ½ C. sour cream
- ¾ C. shredded Swiss cheese
- 36 jumbo pasta shells (about 12 oz.)
- ¼ C. butter
- 1 C. sliced mushrooms, optional
- ½ C. chopped green onion
- 3 cloves garlic, minced
- ¼ C. flour
- ¼ C. white wine, optional
- 1 tsp. salt
- ½ tsp. pepper
- 2 C. half & half (or milk)
- 1 C. shredded Parmesan cheese

In a large saucepan of simmering water, cook shrimp until pink and opaque, about 2 minutes. Drain; cut each shrimp in thirds and place in a bowl. Add sour cream and Swiss cheese, stirring to combine.

Preheat oven to 375°. Lightly coat a 9 x 13" baking dish with cooking spray. In a large pot of lightly salted boiling water, cook pasta shells as directed on package until cooked through, but still firm to the bite, about 13 minutes. Gently remove shells with a slotted spoon. Stuff 18 cooked shells with shrimp mixture and place in prepared baking dish. Cover each stuffed shell with another shell to enclose the filling.

In a skillet over medium heat, melt butter. Add mushrooms, onion and garlic; sauté about 3 minutes. Stir in flour, wine, salt, pepper and half & half. Cook, stirring constantly, until thickened and smooth. Pour sauce over stuffed shells and sprinkle with Parmesan cheese. Bake about 25 minutes or until cheese has melted and begins to brown and sauce is bubbling. Keep warm to serve.

Note: You may substitute small precooked frozen shrimp or use 1 lb. shrimp plus 8 oz. small bay scallops.

All I need is a lifeboat!

Recipes

Serves 10

Spinach Salad (Seaweed)

Dressing
- ½ C. sugar
- 2 tsp. minced onion
- ¼ C. white wine vinegar
- ¼ C. cider vinegar
- ½ C. vegetable oil
- ¼ tsp. paprika
- 2 T. toasted sesame seeds*

Salad Mixture
- 1 (3.75 oz.) pkg. oven or honey roasted sliced almonds (such as Almond Accents)
- 1 lb. fresh spinach, rinsed, torn into pieces
- 1 (6 oz.) pkg. dried sweetened cranberries
- 1 (11 oz.) can mandarin oranges, drained

In a medium bowl, whisk together sugar, onion, wine vinegar, cider vinegar, oil, paprika and sesame seeds; cover and chill dressing until serving time.

In a large bowl, combine spinach, almonds, cranberries and oranges. Just before serving, lightly toss dressing and salad mixture together.

* To toast, place sesame seeds in a single layer in a dry skillet over medium heat or on a baking sheet in a 350° oven for approximately 10 minutes or until golden brown.

Somebody rescue me!

SOS

Recipes

Serves 9

Pineapple Upside-Down Cake
(Sunken Treasure)

¼ C. plus ⅓ C. butter, divided
⅔ C. brown sugar
⅓ C. light corn syrup
9 pineapple slices, drained
9 maraschino cherries, no stems, drained

1⅓ C. flour
1 C. sugar
1½ tsp. baking powder
½ tsp. salt
¾ C. milk
1 egg

Preheat oven to 350°. In a 9″ square baking pan, melt ¼ cup butter in oven. Sprinkle brown sugar evenly over butter; drizzle with syrup. Arrange pineapple slices on top, in rows of three. Place a cherry in the center of each slice.

In a medium mixing bowl, beat together flour, sugar, remaining ⅓ cup butter, baking powder, salt, milk and egg for about 3 minutes. Pour batter over pineapple and cherries. Bake for 50 to 55 minutes or until cake tests done with a toothpick. Immediately place a heatproof serving plate upside down over pan; turn plate and pan over. Leave pan in place for a few minutes before removing. Cut between pineapple slices into squares; serve warm.

Do-ahead tip: Cut pieces and place on dessert plates. Before serving, reheat in the microwave.

Embrace the theme

A "message in a bottle" invitation is perfect for this party. Print your invitations on tea-stained paper, roll up tightly with rubber bands and slide into clean glass or plastic bottles (like recycled beverage bottles). Hand-deliver the invitations to your guests.

If weather permits, eat outdoors on a patio or deck. Create a tropical paradise with patio lights and tiki torches around a fire pit. Hang up treasure maps and charts. Display any of these items (enlarged images or real) to add to the mood: boats, thatched huts, grass skirts, tribal masks, primitive spears, palm and coconut trees or other island props.

Haunted Halloween!

What's for dinner?   A.K.A.

Roasted Pumpkin Seeds	Jack's Remains
Orange Punch	Twilight Tonic
Celery Sticks	Snapped Ribs
Baby-cut Carrots	6 Inches Under
BBQ Ribs	Spare Parts
Potato Skins	Shriveled Flesh
Cole Slaw	Shredded Heads
Garlic Bread	Vampire's Dread
Dirt Cupcakes	Coffin's Cover
Raspberry Iced Tea	Witch's Brew
Drinking Straw	Witching Stick
Fork	Devil's Tongue
Knife	In Your Back
Napkin	Ogre Sleeve
Toothpick	Elm Corpse

8 guests

Make 2 copies of matching menu for each guest *(back of book)*

46

Make this party howl!

Think of slightly spooky haunted graveyards and curiously creepy body parts – that's what fills this Halloween menu. Your guests will choose foods in three separate courses, using only the "Also Known As" code names. **Get ready for a spirited meal and frightful fun!**

Come to a Mystery Meal

Food Prep **Day Before**

Roasted Pumpkin Seeds (Jack's Remains): Roast pumpkin seeds, page 48. Store in an airtight container.

Celery Sticks (Snapped Ribs): Wash 5 celery stalks and cut each into 4 pieces. Chill overnight.

Cole Slaw (Shredded Heads): Mix a 14-oz. bag shredded cabbage with your favorite cole slaw dressing. Cover and chill overnight.

Dirt Cupcakes (Coffin's Cover): Bake and decorate cupcakes, page 51.

Food Prep **Party Day**

BBQ Ribs (Spare Parts): Prepare ribs, starting 3-4 hours before mealtime, page 49. Keep warm.

Orange Punch (Twilight Tonic): Mix and chill punch, page 49.

Witch's Brew: Prepare 2 qts. iced tea using instant tea powder or tea bags. Pour over ice to serve.

Baby-cut Carrots (6 Inches Under): Rinse and chill a 16-oz. bag baby-cut carrots.

Potato Skins (Shriveled Flesh): Prepare and bake potato skins, page 50. Garnish and serve warm.

Garlic Bread (Vampire's Dread): Bake a purchased loaf of sliced garlic bread according to package directions. Serve warm.

Don't Forget

✓ Photocopy menu *(2 per guest)*

✓ Decorate table

✓ Make a label for each menu item *(real name plus code name)*

✓ Organize food service area

Dish it Up

Collect one completed Halloween menu from each guest. Dish up only one course at a time using this guide to determine serving sizes:

Pumpkin Seeds: ¼ cup
Punch: 6-8 ounces
Celery: 2 pieces
Carrots: 3-4 carrots
BBQ Ribs: 1 portion

Potato Skins: 2 skins
Cole Slaw: ½ cup
Garlic Bread: 1 slice
Cupcakes: 1 cupcake
Iced Tea: 8 ounces

Recipes

Roasted Pumpkin Seeds
(Jack's Remains)

Serves 10

5 T. sugar, divided
¼ tsp. ground cumin
¼ tsp. ground cinnamon
¼ tsp. ground ginger
¼ tsp. cayenne pepper
2½ C. pumpkin seeds, rinsed, dried
2 tsp. salt
1 T. olive oil

Preheat oven to 300°. Line a baking sheet with parchment paper. In a large bowl, mix 3 tablespoons sugar, cumin, cinnamon, ginger and cayenne pepper; set aside. Place pumpkin seeds on prepared pan, spray with cooking spray and sprinkle with salt. Bake until lightly browned, 20 to 25 minutes.

Heat oil in a large nonstick skillet over medium heat. Stir in toasted seeds and remaining 2 tablespoons sugar. Cook and stir for 2 to 3 minutes or until caramelized. Add seeds to sugar-spice mixture in bowl and toss to coat. Cool before serving.

Recipes

Orange Punch (Twilight Tonic)

Serves 12

46 oz. pineapple juice
1 (14 oz.) can sweetened condensed milk
2 L orange soda
4 scoops orange sherbet, optional

In a punch bowl or large beverage jug, mix pineapple juice and sweetened condensed milk. Add orange soda and sherbet, if desired. Stir until well blended. Pour over ice to serve.

BBQ Ribs (Spare Parts)

Serves 10

4½ lbs. pork spareribs
¾ C. brown sugar
¼ C. ketchup
¼ C. soy sauce
¼ C. Worcestershire sauce
1 T. vanilla extract
½ C. chile sauce
2 cloves garlic, minced
1 tsp. dry mustard
Dash of pepper

Preheat oven to 350°. Cut spareribs into serving portions and wrap in a double layer of foil. Bake for 1½ hours.

Remove from oven, unwrap and drain. Line a large roasting pan with foil; place ribs in pan. In a bowl, mix brown sugar, ketchup, soy sauce, Worcestershire sauce, vanilla, chile sauce, garlic, dry mustard and pepper. Coat ribs with sauce mixture. Cover pan and marinate at room temperature for up to 1 hour.

To cook, preheat oven to 350°. Bake ribs in pan for 30 minutes, basting several times with marinade during cooking. Keep warm until serving.

Do-ahead tip: Ribs may be pre-cooked in foil and then marinated in a covered pan in the refrigerator overnight. Increase final cooking time slightly.

Recipes

Serves 10

Potato Skins (Shriveled Flesh)

10 baking potatoes, scrubbed
⅓ C. vegetable or olive oil
2 T. grated Parmesan cheese
1 tsp. coarse salt
½ tsp. garlic powder
½ tsp. paprika
¼ tsp. pepper
3 C. shredded Cheddar cheese
12 strips bacon, cooked, crumbled
1 C. sour cream
1 bunch green onions, sliced

Preheat oven to 400°. Prick potato skins and bake for 45 to 50 minutes or until tender. Remove from oven and increase oven temperature to 475°.
Slice baked potatoes in half lengthwise. Scoop out pulp, leaving a shell at least ¼" thick; reserve pulp for another use. Set hollowed-out skins on a lightly greased baking sheet. In a small bowl, mix oil, Parmesan cheese, salt, garlic powder, paprika and pepper; brush lightly over both sides of skins. Bake for 7 minutes, turn skins over and bake for 7 minutes more or until crisp. Sprinkle Cheddar cheese and bacon inside skins. Return to oven for 2 minutes or until cheese is melted. Keep warm to serve. Garnish with sour cream and onions just before serving.

Do-ahead tip: Bake potatoes and cook bacon the day before party. Assemble and bake skins on party day.

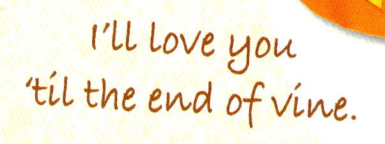

I'll love you 'til the end of vine.

50

Recipes

Serves 24

Dirt Cupcakes (Coffin's Cover)

1 (18.25 oz.) pkg. devil's food cake mix
1⅓ C. buttermilk
½ C. vegetable oil
3 eggs
1 (12 oz.) pkg. semi-sweet chocolate chips (2 C.)
1 C. caramel topping
1 C. prepared chocolate frosting
1 C. crushed chocolate cookies

Preheat oven to 350°. Line muffin pans with Halloween paper liners. In a large mixing bowl, beat together cake mix, buttermilk, oil and eggs on low speed for 30 seconds. Increase speed and beat for 2 minutes. Pour batter into liners, filling about ⅔ full. Sprinkle chocolate chips over batter. Bake for 20 to 25 minutes or until cupcakes test done. Cool 20 minutes.

Spray a meat fork with cooking spray. Poke warm cupcakes with fork several times. Slowly pour caramel topping over cupcakes. Cool completely.

Spread frosting on cupcakes and sprinkle with crushed cookies; press lightly to hold. Cover and store at room temperature.

Embrace the theme

To get into the Halloween spirit, ask guests to dress in costume. Decorate the dining area with carved jack-o-lanterns, orange and black streamers, dangling plastic skeletons and spiders, small vampires or ogres, witch hats and brooms, fake graveyard headstones, shovels and other Halloween gear.

Cover tables with black or orange tablecloths. Add to the spook factor with tall, well-used candles in old-fashioned candle holders and a cauldron centerpiece filled with dry ice. Play some creepy Halloween noises in the background.

Fairy Tales

What's for dinner? A.K.A.

What's for dinner?	A.K.A.
Cheese Ball	The Golden Ball
Crackers	Can't Whistle While You Work
Apple Wedges	Snow White's Mistake
Angel Hair Spaghetti	Rapunzel's Gift
Marinara Sauce	Rose Red
Meatball(s)	A Royal Ball
Green Beans	Jack's Ladder
7-Layer Salad	Lumpy Mattress
Crescent Rolls/Butter	Under the Moon's Spell
Pumpkin Dessert	Cinderella's Ride
Punch	Magic Potion
Fork	Dinglehopper
Knife	Knight's Necessity
Spoon	Magic Mirror
Napkin	Sleeping Cousin

8 guests

Make 2 copies of matching menu for each guest *(back of book)*

52

Once Upon a Time

Enjoy fairy tales all over again when you serve guests three courses of food with code names tied to these familiar stories. **Imagine royalty, magic, heroes and love for a very happy ending!**

Food Prep **Day Before**

Cheese Ball (The Golden Ball): Purchase or prepare your favorite cheese ball; chill overnight.

7-Layer Salad (Lumpy Mattress): Assemble salad, page 54. Cover and chill overnight. Toss lightly before serving.

Pumpkin Dessert (Cinderella's Ride): Bake dessert, page 55. Cool completely and refrigerate overnight. Cut before serving.

Crackers (Can't Whistle While You Work): Place 8-10 crackers in snack-size baggie for each guest.

Food Prep **Party Day**

Apple Wedges (Snow White's Mistake): Cut 2 large apples into 8-12 wedges each. Dip in lemon juice to prevent browning.

Angel Hair Spaghetti (Rapunzel's Gift): Cook 2 oz. dry pasta per guest. Toss with butter; serve warm.

Meatball(s) (A Royal Ball): Follow package directions to cook 3-5 small meatballs per guest (or make large homemade meatballs). Keep warm.

Marinara Sauce (Rose Red): Make or purchase about 50 oz. spaghetti sauce. Heat before serving.

Green Beans (Jack's Ladder): Cook fresh, frozen or canned green beans, following package directions. Season and serve warm. (1¾ lb. fresh, 2 (12 oz.) pkgs. frozen or 3 (14.5 oz.) cans)

Crescent Rolls (Under the Moon's Spell): Following package directions, bake 1-2 refrigerated crescent rolls for each guest; serve warm.

Punch (Magic Potion): Serve any punch over ice in glasses (2 L needed).

Don't Forget

✓ Photocopy menu *(2 per guest)*
✓ Decorate table
✓ Make a label for each menu item *(real name plus code name)*
✓ Organize food service area

Dish it Up

Collect one completed Fairy Tales menu from each guest. Dish up only one course at a time using this guide to determine serving sizes:

Cheese Ball: 1-2 tablespoons

Crackers: 1 baggie

Apple Wedges: 2-3 wedges

Spaghetti: about 1 cup

Marinara Sauce: ½ cup

Meatball(s): 1 large or 3-5 small

Green Beans: about ½ cup

Layered Salad: about 1 cup

Crescent Rolls: 1-2 rolls

Pumpkin Dessert: 1 piece

Punch: 8 ounces

Recipes

7-Layer Salad (Lumpy Mattress)

Serves 12

- 4 C. chopped lettuce, divided
- 2 C. torn spinach leaves, divided
- Salt and pepper to taste
- 6 hard-cooked eggs, sliced
- 2 C. frozen peas, partially thawed
- 12 oz. bacon, cooked, crumbled
- 2 C. shredded Cheddar cheese
- ½ C. mayonnaise
- ½ C. sour cream
- 1 to 2 T. sugar
- ¼ C. thinly sliced green onion
- Paprika

In a large bowl, place half the lettuce and spinach. Sprinkle with salt and pepper. Layer egg slices on top. Continue to layer ingredients in this order: peas, remaining lettuce and spinach, bacon and cheese; season as desired.

In a small bowl, mix mayonnaise, sour cream and sugar. Spread over salad to cover. Cover and chill overnight.

Before serving, top with onion and paprika; toss lightly.

Recipes

Serves 18

Pumpkin Dessert
(Cinderella's Ride)

- 1 (15 oz.) can pumpkin
- 3 eggs
- 4 tsp. pumpkin pie spice
- 1 (12 oz.) can evaporated milk
- 1 C. sugar
- 1 (18.25 oz.) pkg. yellow or butter pecan cake mix
- ½ C. butter, melted
- ¾ C. chopped pecans, walnuts or cashews
- Whipped topping

Preheat oven to 350°. Coat a 9 x 13" cake pan with cooking spray. In a large bowl, stir together pumpkin, eggs, spice, evaporated milk and sugar until well blended. Pour into prepared pan. Sprinkle dry cake mix on top. Drizzle melted butter over the top and sprinkle with nuts. Bake for 45 minutes or until set, covering lightly with foil for the last 10 minutes if browning too quickly. Let cool. Cut into pieces and top with whipped topping.

Do-ahead tip: To make serving easy, plate each piece before the meal.

Embrace the theme

★ Welcome guests of all ages to step into a land of enchantment when you create a royal castle with white twinkle lights, yards of pink and white tulle, fake jewels, fairy dust (A.K.A. glitter), magic wands, fake swords and all things glitzy. Give guests inexpensive crowns, tiaras or cone-shaped hats to wear during the party. Use streamers to decorate chairs like thrones. Hang paper pennants on clothesline to define party area.

★ Display fairy tale movie posters and children's books to get conversations going. Everyone loves happily-ever-after endings!

Olé! Celebrate a Mexican Fiesta Mystery Meal!

This Mexican party features a menu filled with delicious south-of-the-border foods using deceptive code names. Your meal will be served in three separate courses. Using the menu's code names on the left, choose foods, beverages, eating utensils and a napkin, writing them in the order you'd like things to be served. You must put one code name in each blank to the right and use every menu item once — no duplicates or skips allowed. Use your Spanish know-how and clever thinking to decode the menu **for a fiesta worth celebrating!**

Your Name _____

1st Course (Please pick any 4 items.)

_____
_____
_____
_____

What's for dinner?

Mexican Flag	Cactus
Shared Siesta	Pitted Out
Salty Dance	Chick Under a Poncho
Sweet Soap	Dressed Pony
Zorro	Beans & Bark
Tipsy Sombrero	Matador's Cape

2nd Course (Please pick any 4 items.)

_____
_____
_____
_____

3rd Course (Please pick any 4 items.)

_____
_____
_____
_____

Howdy Partner! It's a Wild West Mystery Meal!

Cookie's been rustlin' up a full menu of gut-pleasin' grub, though you might not recognize a single food by these confounded nicknames. Your meal will be served in four courses. Using the menu's code names below, choose foods, beverages, eating utensils and a napkin, writing them in the order you'd like things to be served. You must put one code name in each blank below and use every menu item once – no duplicates or skips allowed.
Round up the posse to find the clues – it's time for a showdown at the old ranch.

Your Name _____

What's for dinner?

Pitch It
Smokin' Guns
Big Dipper
Chew on This
Squealing Bedrolls

Underground Tap
Rustler's Game
Boot Fruit
Cowboy Joe
Slop Stopper

Whittle a Little
Saddlesore & Salve
Rootin' Tootin' Cowboy
Panning for Gold
Trigger's Old Age Treat

1st Course (Please pick any 4 items.)

_____
_____
_____
_____

2nd Course (Please pick any 4 items.)

_____
_____
_____
_____

3rd Course (Please pick any 4 items.)

_____
_____
_____
_____

4th Course (Please pick any 3 items.)

_____
_____
_____

Get Groovin' With a Classic Rock and Roll Mystery Meal!

It's time to rock and roll with classic favorites in music and food. This meal will be served in three courses. Using the menu's nicknames on the left, choose foods, beverages, eating utensils and a napkin, writing them in the order you'd like things to be served. You must put one nickname in each blank to the right and use every menu item once — no duplicates or skips allowed. Tune into the clues and turn on to a rocking good time!

Your Name _____

What's for dinner?

American Pie
Groovin' on a Sunday Afternoon
Tutti Frutti
Will It Go Round in Circles
Black Water
Whole Lotta Shakin' Goin' On
It's Only Rock and Roll
Wipeout
Hot Fun in the Summertime
Light My Fire
Happy Together
Pick up the Pieces
Cold as Ice
Come Together
Love Bites

1st Course (Please pick any 5 items.)

_____
_____
_____
_____
_____

2nd Course (Please pick any 5 items.)

_____
_____
_____
_____
_____

3rd Course (Please pick any 5 items.)

_____
_____
_____
_____
_____

RELAX AND ENJOY THIS TROPICAL LUAU MYSTERY MEAL!

Soft island breezes and delectable tropical foods greet you at this luau. Your meal will be served in three courses. Using the menu's nicknames on the left, choose foods, beverages, eating utensils and a napkin, writing them in the order you'd like things to be served. You must put one nickname in each blank to the right and use every menu item once — no duplicates or skips allowed. **Look for hints to reveal each nickname. Then hang loose and enjoy the show!**

Your Name _____

What's for dinner?

Opposites Attract
Island Fight
Monkey Money
Imitation Pearls
Chillin' on the Beach
Grains of Sand
Two Tickets to Paradise
Sweet Spit
Lei in Lap
Tiki Time
Do the Rumba
Dip in the Rip

1st Course (Please pick any 4 items.)
_____
_____
_____
_____

2nd Course (Please pick any 4 items.)
_____
_____
_____
_____

3rd Course (Please pick any 4 items.)
_____
_____
_____
_____

COME TO THE MARDI GRAS MYSTERY MEAL!

Enjoy a rollicking Louisiana carnival to celebrate Fat Tuesday. This Cajun-style meal will be served in three courses. Using the menu's code names on the left, choose foods, beverages, eating utensils and a napkin, writing them in the order you'd like things to be served. You must put one code name in each blank to the right and use every menu item once — no duplicates or skips allowed. You'll need some good luck to unmask these disguised menu names. **Get ready to party!**

Your Name _____

What's for dinner?

Tuned Up
Going Nuts
Wind & Water
Masker
Bayou Crunch
Carnival Cut-up
Fat Tuesday
Melting Pot
New Orleans Special
Mix it Up
Crescent City Crush
Fit for Royalty
French Quarter Loafer
Get the Scoop

1st Course (Please pick any 5 items.)
_____
_____
_____
_____
_____

2nd Course (Please pick any 5 items.)
_____
_____
_____
_____
_____

3rd Course (Please pick any 4 items.)
_____
_____
_____
_____

get lucky in love with this romantic mystery meal

Celebrate love and romance when you enjoy three courses of decadent foods. Using the menu's lovey-dovey nicknames on the left, choose foods, beverages, eating utensils and a napkin, writing them in the order you'd like things to be served. You must put one nickname in each blank to the right and use every menu item once – no duplicates or skips allowed. Use your head and heart to decode these nicknames. **Then dim the lights and get swept away!**

Your Name _____

What's for dinner?

You Make My Head Spin
Keep it Clean
"I pick you!"
Chilling Out Together
Hot Couple
Tie the Knot
Cupid's Arrow
Use It or Lose It
Heart's Desire
Hot & Steamy
Wine & Dine
Cuddling
24 Karat Rings
Cut to the Chase
Love Pats

1st Course (Please pick any 5 items.)
_____
_____
_____
_____
_____

2nd Course (Please pick any 5 items.)
_____
_____
_____
_____
_____

3rd Course (Please pick any 5 items.)
_____
_____
_____
_____
_____

SOS! Rescued at the Shipwreck Island Mystery Meal!

Your ship may be wrecked but the food will be a real treasure. This meal will be served in three courses. Using the menu's code names on the left, choose foods, beverages, eating utensils and a napkin, writing them in the order you'd like things to be served. You must put one code name in each blank to the right and use every menu item once — no duplicates or skips allowed. **Explore the clues in the code names to enjoy the mysteries of this deserted island!**

Your Name _____

What's for dinner?

Seaweed	Liquid Gold
Harpoon	Oil Slick
Oar	Grouchy Castaways
Sunken Treasure	Float Your Boat
Sponge	Net
Splinter	Swashbuckler
Sea Shells	Fish Bait

1st Course (Please pick any 5 items.)
_____
_____
_____
_____
_____

2nd Course (Please pick any 5 items.)
_____
_____
_____
_____
_____

3rd Course (Please pick any 4 items.)
_____
_____
_____
_____

Velcome to the Haunted Halloween Mystery Meal!

You'll find delectable body parts and ghostly favorites on this menu! The meal will be served in three courses. Using the menu's code names on the left, choose foods, beverages, eating utensils and a napkin, writing them in the order you'd like things to be served. You must put one code name in each blank to the right and use every menu item once — no duplicates or skips allowed. Use your sixth sense to decipher these creepy code names for a frightfully fun time!

Your Name _____

What's for dinner?

- Coffin's Cover
- In Your Back
- Jack's Remains
- Vampire's Dread
- Elm Corpse
- Twilight Tonic
- Shredded Heads
- Snapped Ribs
- Witching Stick
- 6 Inches Under
- Shriveled Flesh
- Devil's Tongue
- Ogre Sleeve
- Spare Parts
- Witch's Brew

1st Course (Please pick any 5 items.)
_____
_____
_____
_____
_____

2nd Course (Please pick any 5 items.)
_____
_____
_____
_____
_____

3rd Course (Please pick any 5 items.)
_____
_____
_____
_____
_____

Be enchanted with a Fairy Tale Mystery Meal

Step back in time to the land of enchantment where princesses find true love and heroes are born. This meal will be served in three courses. Using the menu's nicknames on the left, choose foods, beverages, eating utensils and a napkin, writing them in the order you'd like things to be served. You must put one nickname in each blank to the right and use every menu item once— no duplicates or skips allowed. Your fairy tale memories can help you reveal the true identity of each menu item. Get ready for a happy ending!

Your Name _____

What's for dinner?

- Cinderella's Ride
- Rose Red
- Magic Mirror
- Can't Whistle While You Work
- Magic Potion
- Snow White's Mistake
- A Royal Ball
- Knight's Necessity
- The Golden Ball
- Rapunzel's Gift
- Dinglehopper
- Under the Moon's Spell
- Sleeping Cousin
- Jack's Ladder
- Lumpy Mattress

1st Course (Please pick any 5 items.)

_____
_____
_____
_____
_____

2nd Course (Please pick any 5 items.)

_____
_____
_____
_____
_____

3rd Course (Please pick any 5 items.)

_____
_____
_____
_____
_____